Seven Portholes In Hell

HOLOCAUST LIBRARY

Statement of Purpose

The Holocaust spread across the face of Europe almost fifty years ago. The brutality then unleashed is still nearly beyond comprehension. Millions of innocents, men, women and children, were consumed by its flames.

The goal of Holocaust Library, a non-profit organization founded by survivors, is to publish and disseminate works on the Holocaust. These will include survivors' accounts, testimonies and memoirs, historical and regional analyses, anthologies, archival and source documents and other relevant materials that will help shed light on this cataclysmic era.

These books and studies will be made available to the general public, scholars, researchers, historians, teachers and students. They will be used in Holocaust Resource Centers, libraries and schools, synagogues and churches. They will help foster an increased awareness of the Holocaust and its implications. They will help *to preserve the memory* for posterity and to enable this awesome time to be better understood and comprehended.

SEVEN PORTHOLES IN HELL

Poems of the Holocaust

by
Asher Torren

HOLOCAUST LIBRARY
New York

Library of Congress Cataloging-in-Publication Data

Torren, Asher. 1936-

    Seven portholes in hell: poems of the Holocaust / Asher Torren.
      p.   cm.
    ISBN 0-89604-150-6 (cloth): $18.95.—ISBN 0-89604-151-4
    (paper): $9.95
    1. Holocaust, Jewish (1939-1945)—Poetry. I. Title.
    PS3570.0695S48   1991   91-7169
    811'.54—dc20   CIP

Cover Design by The Appelbaum Company
Printed in the United States

For Rachel Gimpelovsky and Montefiore Turgeman

Contents

Acknowledgments

Thanks to the following magazines in which some of these poems first appeared: Archer, Art:Mag, Bitterroot, Dog River Review, Fennel Stalk, Gypsy, Hob-Nob, Impetus, Jewish Chronicle, Late Knocking, Legerete, The Mage, Midwest Poetry Review, Mind In Motion, Negative Capability, Orphic Lute, Piedmont Literary Review, Prophetic Voices, Reconstructionist, Ripples, Sepia, Sou'-wester, Touchstone, Voices-Israel and Z. Miscellaneous. Thanks also to Marcia Rosenberg and Terry Hayes for their painstaking assistance, Margalit Levine for her timely suggestions and to the Research Foundation of the City University of New York for the PSC-CUNY, Creative Incentive Award.

I. HOLOCAUST

1939-45

When my eyes see
But fail to recognize
I wrap my soul
With dark clouds
And then I know
Why this hand
Writes about the gallows . . .
The dead couldn't.

After The Fire

Reader, what can I give you?
What is left for us
Is not within my grasp.

Should you think it is,
Insist on further proof,
I did; I still do.

If what is left behind
Is the light,
You and I share custody of it,
But bluntly, desperately,
You may be it.

Inside The Cave

Inside the cave inmates huddle, listening
To the volcano squeeze the rocks.
Restless feet dart in and out . . .

Crushed, when the cave lost,
When the good life changed allegiance,
And passion resigned.

In shame,
Not a prayer came out,
Just a parched whisper crying:

Ask me what an early death is
Under the lava flow.

Ask me while my hands
Tremble and stitch these
Empty pages for you.

A Holocaust Poem

When I walked off the train
I was judged. Naked,
Dispirited, on the ramp
To the gas chamber,
I was judged.

Verdicts, painful verdicts,
Bled me down, back to the past,
Our common stinking past,
Where the sum of all was zero
And my god was unaware.

Off the road I sit
Reflecting the pyre's glow.
I sit, I judge.

12/89

Behind The Door

I brought death with me
In a chest that yearned for deeds,
But the Gauleiter had his orders,
The ground must be cut clear.

I never wanted to go on and on
Nurturing death within; a nursery
For the growing pain of knowing;
A vault for a virus in retreat.

I was driven to outrun
The smell of gangrenous limbs,
The burst appendix' pain, but
Perplexed, my ledger was left behind.

I ran fast on the short track,
Clothed, then naked; ignorant, then learned.
I counted milestones when anniversaries failed,
When speed rejected the encroachment of time.

I brought death with me
Into this windowless atelier,
Where I lived my life and died without tears,
Without bleeding, without growing old.

11/16/89

The Past

When the evening rushes to expire
And I walk through the door,
This door, any door,
Is the past waiting?

With time aging at my breasts,
And friends, unknowingly, taking
Their last leave, I feel
The stranger in the womb.

Hard, explosive, sharing no plans;
A relentless pause crouching,
Waiting for words to come alive.

A relentless pause looking for
A tiny flash to light the distant eye.

A relentless pause shrinking
. . . and passing through.

And when I wake up
In the darkness of that distant glow,
Will I hear the cutting of new flesh,
The shuffle of busy feet and
A muffled voice beyond the portal
Crying, "Mommy, Mommy."

Look Up Sad Cyclamen

What can be done with unused embraces?
Reassurances for solemn buds
Thumbing rides to the spotlight?

Left behind, in the shadows
Of half-buried rocks,
Newly hammered amulets
Power a longer descent.

Frantic planning behind blank looks
Stir gentle dusting from our hearts, and
Silver slivers from the wet sky
Uselessly bounce off the lens.

Walk down the blind streets one more time.
Rich smells roll by; yesterday's witnesses
Escort you back to the garden.

Look up sad cyclamen.
Admiring eyes paint the air
That touches you—fitted for you.

The peace you made with the rocks
Protects you—go on sad cyclamen,
Flatter the light with your crown.

Look up at the clouds,
Forming, passing, dissipating;
Look up and blow farewells
For your children below.

Auschwitz Diary

I am sinking into a meaningless pit
Thinking of food.

I'm passing from life to non-life
To be a diary of words that never surfaced;
A diary of gray, angular time and sameness;
A diary of long-incarcerated senseless fears.

I am passing without leaving a record
With every thud of my hunger pangs.

I claw through nothingness, untouched
By dripping crumbs of emaciated kindness.

I planned to include translations and illustrations
But my thoughts drifted back to suet.

I planned to include references to my past,
To proud achievements, but memories
Could not surpass my presence here.

Diary! I cannot sustain you.
Without words, without a source,
What am I but molecules.

11/16/89

In The Gas Chamber

I envy the words, the shiny
Buttons of our splendid costume.

I envy the words that escaped,
I envy their fleetness and easy truths.

I envy the words before
The tears and screams begin;

When our love is thriving
Behind the door.

You and me, alone,
Squeezed naked in the dark;

You and me and the beauty
Of love awakened.

You and me, unsullied
By time and doubt,

You and me, unsullied
By words and their easy,
Fleeting truths, you and me.

6/89

11

The Doomed

Whose ashes came up
When the spade struck bone,
When the hilltops quivered and split?

Whose gaze bore fruit
When the faithless grew enamored,
When the deaf-mutes' aim intensified?

Unbloodied, their wedding best glistened,
Their time together sublime. Ah . . .

Uncover His name and purify time,
In being, in giving . . . in unison:
"Oh, greatness, greatness arriving!"
Sighed the doomed.

Cloudseeding

Low fly-by in the Polish skies.
Foreskinned smokestacks spew forth
Sooty, blind spermatids cloudseeding
The vacant chuppa over Auschwitz.

I scan the smoky rubble below,
Through piled skeletons and toys,
Looking for the promised mate.

The head-up display flickers senseless signals
Unmatched with the dental records
Strapped to my lap. In panic,

I slam my impotence into the ashen fields
To penetrate the core of the growing disorder,
To penetrate the eviscerated bellies
Of Leah and Feige, daughters of Dinnah,
And others whose names slipped away
From my mother's eroded memory.

Raindrops, moist crystal embryos,
And seeds of marigolds and sunflowers,
Refuse the offer!
Let the wind that spins the face of the earth
Carry the life you make
To another sky, another soil,
Away from the sealed grimace of this landfill,
Away from stilled time back at zero.

2/18/89

13

To Holocaust Centrum

Off the train at a slow bend
I tumble and roll, my viscera,
Tugging at their moorings,
Thump audible thanks for the chance
To walk this incinerator-bound, endless track.

I walk with a python seven-coiled
Around my neck, hissing into my ear:
You've stayed too long, you have it coming.

Homeless words sprint off my lips,
The blink of the eye becomes a momentous pursuit
And steering-in a course correction,
A venture into the dropping unknown.

This is the time before the ram,
A time of disbelief, for he,
Who walked out many times before
Is on his feet again.

4/89

Sonderkommando

Do not wipe the semen off your hands, Leo—
Not the excrement, not the blood of women.
Let us live a little longer
While our bodies burn.

Run back for another load, Leo.
We are with you from the start
Of the next turn of the wheel.

We are with you, Leo,
While our particles churn in the stinking air.

With you, Leo,
When the pace slows down
And settles into our next dream.
We are with you, Leo.

6/89

Thessaloniki Kaput

Mama, why is Papa crying?
Papa has to help with the load
Before he, too, can take a shower.

Carry us, Papa,
Carry Mama in your arms,
Like the cargo in the Port.

Two sacks at the time;
Forty kilos of burlapped wheat
From the launch to the ramp,
To unload the ship before Shabbat,
Before Thessaloniki washed itself clean
And lit the gentle lights.

Do not cry, Papa.
Do not hesitate because our eyes are open.
We are clean and ready, Papa.
We are waiting to be moved.

6/89

El Tango Fabuloso

Among the 90,000 bodies unearthed and burned in
Ponary, Ely the Black recognized his wife and
daughter.

You always passed out
When I held you so close,
When every tango was
Our first and last.

Limed, putrid figure
I dug you out,
Smothered Ponary quarry,
Cut marble of my eyes.

Let us glide again, then turn,
Before I torch your body
Good-bye, and go on
Wedded to our tango,
Shackled to the pit
You left behind.

Judenrat(1)

Trapped ahead of the red tide rolling,
Trapped in sight of a million kulaks dying,
Trapped under flying echelons stumping,
I pour imprisoned languor out for you.

Sweetheart, sweet Brunhilde,
I loft kisses for your breasts,
Enflamed circles of desire, and run
Amok through cut-off Rudnicka Street
To catch a transport to Birkenau.

Brilliantined and razor-sharp
In a brown double-breasted suit
I shut the blind vermin out,
And enter the chamber, commissioned,
Entrusted.

Oh Goethe! O Richard! Oh noble kin!
Let me into your bed tonight.

Dry-mouthed, I kiss the serpent's lips
And blink farewell to you, to you . . .
To new passion throbbing,
To unfortunate odors mounting,
To rejected groins puffing,
Majestically shading my cooling body.

8/88

Judenrat(2)

In his absence
A suspected truant

We bow
To nature's course

And approach the ramp
Anointed

To cleanse
Foretold excesses

The land's fat
Usurped,

Rendered
And saponified.

11/88

Judenrat(3)

Speak to me
For the people

My dreams
Choiceless, time-drained
Sprawl agape

God
You came back . . .
On a postage stamp
Numerals canceled

Surpassed, we huddle
Breathless
At the dark bottom

The dust, chosen
Tallied, one
Duty, three
Tally, slash.

11/88

Shivah Eshnabim BaTophet
(Seven Portholes In Hell)

Meet me behind Block 24, after roll call.
Did you bring the bread?

That's all?
Pick up your skirt.

Stand still!
Stand still . . .

I am choking on the bread,
It is so dry . . . *psia krew!*

The dogs are coming, let go!
Let go, *chulera!* Run . . .

Come back when they are gone.
Will you have more bread?

*　*　*

Next time get one from the kitchen, Hans,
They are fatter and with fewer boils.

A Jewess will starve
but keep her bottom clean.

The rotten Ukrainians drink every night,
Then shoot the best.

Ah, good ones come in every day.
A woman can get very bony

But her breasts stay.
She hated me, I could tell,

Yet, she smiled and got wet.
Everybody learns.

*   *   *

Inmates! First, your life
Was in your mother's hands,

Then you went into the synagogue
And gave God a shot at it,

Then your leaders came in
For a piece of the action,

Now you are here,
And as you can see

Escape is impossible,
Only work to do

And orders to follow.
Hang these miserable criminals!

*   *   *

Hunger and beating make possible
Fast acceptance of synchronization

Between our duty
And our personal feelings.

For them it is we
Who do the dirty work,

For us it is our Führer,
Who helps us overcome

Objectionable tasks,
Difficult tasks. Thank you.

*   *   *

I was not as pretty as my sisters,
Honey-blond, dark-blue eyes . . .

Both went to the left,
Mirele with two infants.

You are pretty if you want to be.
I made myself pretty on the line.

The doctor knew I wanted to live.
They shave your head

On the way to Birkenau.
Here, at least, we have nice underwear,

And sometimes coffee.
I pray every day not to conceive.

With this food you can't even bleed.
The two Russian girls, yes,

Are gone.
They were getting big.

*   *   *

Call his wife and tell her
We cannot come.

Some trouble with the Jews.
Who can eat in this stench, anyway.

I do not like their cook.
He steals food, too.

Everybody steals from the kitchen.
The kids like to be driven to the gate.

They like the towers and the dogs.
That is no place for children.

*　*　*

Mommy, I had a dream:
The train is going through the trees

In the mountains,
And raindrops trickle on my hair.

The cool air is striking my face.
I heard big birds calling each other,

And then the bells woke me up.
Did you hear me?

Wake up, Mommy, I had a dream.
Wake up, Mommy, wake up!

Go back to sleep, little girl.
No use crying, now.

7/89

Leibel Gimpelovsky

I am not named after you,
My son is.
When your sister needed
A name,
Yours was still yours.

Hungry partisans of
The frozen forest
Sent you to bring food
From the Polacks, who
Gave your sleeping body
To shooting Germans.

Your orphaned name,
Fluttering in the cold cellar,
Was left splintered for me.

Reb Nachman's Chair

We file through the narrow enclosure.
Our skins undress to cleanse, to stop
The booted nails and wooded rifle butts.

Doing good, Rebbe, shivering
On the ramp, the bridge
Between the uncertain and the irrelevant.

Above, your chair is flying to the Sacred Land,
Piece by piece, with stealth, cunning and nerve,
While we soil ourselves, shamelessly.

Sweet Rebbe, our love!
Your children, who did not plan to be wise
Nor wicked, face a narrow bridge indeed.

Caught gazing into silenced books and storm-shut ark,
We wait for traditions to rise and heal our sores.
We pray for your golden tears to light our moment
On our way to the showers.

Wide eyed, we peek through the closing doors and
Choking contempt. We see our discarded garments
Turn back dejected, and our chastened shadows
Slipping away, perplexed.

1986

Marconi At Ponary

Bring no words
To Ponary

No words
No sounds

No dots
No dashes.

On the pyre
The heat

Sears our transmitters
Shut forever,

And our last words
Burn tracelessly

Three thousand
At a time.

Bodyless, we take
To the skyway

To seek shelter
From the heat

Inside Uranus' tilted rings,
Pitched across the ecliptic,

Concealed in the light—
Always in the light.

An Astronomer's Lament

On the mountain, rub the elbow
Against the steel, the skin
Knows the feeling. Darkness,
Spitting warning shots through
Tunneled teeth, cloaks the eyes,
But the ears come alive
Listening to the whistles and the chill.

Anticipation, a grand addition to the score,
Tumbles in; food for the slippery fireflies
Mindlessly huddled in the current.

And beauty, sustaining manna
For time yet to float by, pales deeper.
To the chuckles of irreverent galaxies
Expanding so far, so red, so far away.

Vomited again into ceaseless space.
What saddened Hubble? Sleepwalkers
Encroaching on a closed book?
Timekeepers boring into a room
Without a pendulum, on a ball without shade,
Where tiny particles tick away among strangers?

. . . and never, never a good word,
Only the latest glass-strangling, cold
Echoes screaming through the aperture.

6/86

31

Jack-In-The-Box

De-fusing unsuccessful,
Booby-trapped, jack-in-the-box.

Smoke and grit replace
Your supple poise; quick moves —
Look through the palms
For the elusive pulse.

Meeting of the eyes
And aimless thoughts
Cut the cranium in two.

Go under jack-in-the-box,
Go under into the can.

The pain separates the face
From the sheets; the pain
Coaxes your genes to relax,
But skin-grafted voids
Are slow to bear fruit.

You, the neurological wunderkind
With the mystery damaged below,
Squeeze hard . . . harder,
Give us a good come shot.

Deflated, jack-in-the-box.
Go under, into the can.
Memory loss will be your comfort,
And Big Ben's smile your relief.

I Fly

I fly, always.
I fly to sire the same story:
A handgrenade bursting on time,
Fragments rip the sky, and
Bodies left behind, on the ground.

Others stay with heirlooms,
With reliable, destructive faces,
I fly the same course every day,

Fifty, sixty times a day,
A lot less at night,
To urge time on,
To free the slow-turning stones.

And while my ghost
Prowls the wetlands by night,
I give birth by day.

Many days, many starts—same ending:
A handgrenade bursting, fat
Graphic skin disintegrating, on time.

7/89

Orphans

Orphans walk down the aisle in the Holyland.
A match of evil jest
By Jucha the Joker and Baba Yaga the Witch;
An arena for hungry raptors to collide,
Clasp and release, and fertility to await an arrival.

The infant issue, a receiver of genes
Sheathed with dim codes and vestigial disciplines,
Of orphanhood passing on and on; a receiver
Of angry tales and impaired potency dispensed
By careless bystanders looking in.

Where is their self-assured Mediterranean piety
And vision-pumping rush of the rivers of Ashkenaz?

Where is the right-handed cunning
That sustained millennia of rootlessness
At the hells of Atlas and the bosom of wolves?

Where is the immunity that held back
The transplant's rejection until caution ran out?

Perched high with retracted talons, we gaze
Through narrow cuts in the cornea,
Mistaking a bounty of glare for sunshine.

We never see the thin limbs, the distant faces,
The easy crumbs collecting in the bowls.

We never see the flightless dropping from the nest,
Safety chronicles strapped on . . . failing to deploy.

11/88

A Scroll Concealed

These are the words of your sterile mother,
The wasted seamstress from Ravensbruck.

Shorn for bootliners, starved to feed a soldier,
Groomed under the sloganed gates to be
Eurovision's benign diversion from grief
For dead seedlings and storks,
For speared caymans writhing in the mud,
For reluctant bystanders coerced to obey,
For innocence
Deprived by striped strangers in the woods.

Evicted from the colonies,
The troops are in for a house cleaning
Taking the measure of our vigilance:
Forty nine slain in the Killing City,
A million flattened into an anthill in Musa Daag.

And while we die routinely in Ravensbruck,
Yosarian is motionless in Monte Casino
With a shattered hippocampus and a flat theta wave.

Children, learn to walk at night again,
To conquer the fears of darkness and snakes,
To slay, to be merciful and prepared
For a daylight crossing of the Yabok
With your family intact.

Bring back the Teacher from the Mountain
To lay down a trackless path, thin air
For the inquisitive dawn to see, the devil's
Autobahn for your enemies to follow.
Bring back the teacher!

4/2/89

Relay

Visions for wayfarers on a long journey,
Where footing is perilous and
Vigilance is ambiguous company.

Visitors leave the Sinai with
Brand new luggage; practical jokes
For the folks back home.

. . . loss-in-progress along the Via Appia.

In Silesia startled birds dive
Among waterless clouds, and
Everybody is taking time to sleep
When cattle cars roll back empty.

. . . gelded roosters yawning at the gate.

Listen to dark Bavarian forests
Growl back at the wind. See,
Nobody loses a race on the Autobahn,
Where bullet-proof demons search
For a comfortable exit.

The lines at Nazca are straight
And long; stone assemblies and colors
Divided at ground level. Here,
Layered desert varnish guards tales
Only time tells. Sellah.

1985

Polish Transit

When my mother left Poland
She took God with her
To Haifa, Natanya and Brooklyn,
Where He has been doing well.

Awakened empty-handed
Amidst the cold rivers and birch trees,
Amidst the played out past
And the estranged future,
The Perplexed froze.

Guideless, in the flame
Of the burning voice, they moved
To cast their last token
For a short, defiant ride
Through the smokestack.

1986

Look, Look, Look

Look, look, look,
New dimensions struggle
With the gluttonous old; munch,
Munch, munch Hungry Sharks.

Honor to the time-deflated point
And its circle-dancing children.

Accolades to the fleeting placidities
That cashed in everything, you and me,
For another lunge at the surf
And a breathless wriggle on the sand.

The Ape

The ape is worried:
Look at what they are doing here,
You are surely next, he said.

Historically, I began,
Nothing remains the same.
Everything flows . . .

Nothing new here except
A faster current, muttered the ape
And walked away.

7/89

After My Death

I know
The secret of life.
(it is no big deal)
Many died for it,
Others hoped
For a good show;
Words and feelings,
Too remote to be
Of use now,
Too elusive
For the long view.
To be here
And tell the story . . .
To be here
And struggle . . .

The Crash

It began to look crude and vulgar to me to compete
with the surrounding world in creating horrors.
Isak Dinesen, 1943

Where were you when the ground shook?

In that gray, secluded castle
Elegantly sacrificing for us?

Your parts, humming sweet harmony,
Anticipate a breakthrough; perpetuum
Mobile for you and yours,
For pink deserving flesh.

Around, cruel time for everyone,
So many interruptions in the focal plane,

But you, tenaciously sweating it through,
Pasting the finishing touches on
Your Venus de Milo.

1986

On Kiddush HaShem

In the tank farm we grow,
Jews and genes in search of renewal,
Mingling with the colors of the land,
With molecules of wild birds and flowers,
In a union bartered with time.

Flammables, in the pipes from us to you,
Rumble in the rushing darkness,
Bringing oils for the flames of Shabbat,
Bringing life to the consummate few.

Before the covenant with Him expires,
The Consummate climb the Mountain again,
To reenact our Father Abraham's deed,
To stare back at God at high noon.

When the hour of miracles comes
We witness the universe shake,
The earth split open, and
The fire pour out from the open wounds.

Groping in the dark,
The rescue team finds the bodies
Of our son Isaac, Rabbi Amnon, Hanna
And two million children
Splattered on the rocks of Moriah.

With our faith unshaken
We mourn the dead,
And resolve to turn back to green
The blackened hulks of our farm.

We prepare to dissolve
The hardened bloodclots in our pipes
Into flowing, living crimson,
And for now to build a bridge,
A hesitant rainbow,
Touching both His sky and our soil.

Now I Am You

Now I am you, God,
A fire child
On the way up.

I was the fool
Who lost,
A grand total still ascending.

Riding up on seared air
I see a raven circling
Within, saving energy

For the long flight back
To vacant Eden, and
A blind touchdown at dawn.

7/89

A Musar Shtible

I close my eyes to pray:
"If I forget thee, Jerusalem,
Will Novaradock be a just replacement?"

Expelled from comfort and home,
I came to this little house to hide,
To hope—chanting assurances and resolutions,
Through silence and disarray—
For a clear transit through my low.

To you, my teachers, I offer
The serene goodness of a fool,
Putting on, for the first time
And forever, sackcloth and ashes.

With you I wait for a wondrous madness
To settle
In the dimmed interior of my final space.

6/89

Two Days Before
Pearl Harbor

1. Novaradock, Poland, Destroyed

On our own since Forty One,
Twelve, five, nineteen forty one,
The last day of Novaradock,
The day the Final Solution arrived.

Inscribed on Mount Zion's Holocaust Cellar wall:
December fifth, nineteen forty one, Novaradock,
Slashed and burned to fatten the land, anticipating
Tomorrow's hunger pangs.

Our Novaradock, a reminder for the voyager:
We are but hours from the heart; a short,
Choking, umbilical coil away from
Humming molecules enforcing entropy,
And a loss of faith by insurgent critical mass.

Slash and burn, fatten the soil
And race the light, the ghost of the past.
Race and return without glory, betrayed.

Novaradock, a moment's flutter, a delay
In the voyage back to the Rift Valley,
A marker to round at the Perihelion, escape
Velocity unattained; a rendezvous without cause
And effect, without arrogance, without compensation,
Without debt.

Mom and Pop, you couldn't duck the woes of
Weightlessness.

Novaradock, a trading post on the Plain of Indifference;
Unload everything, the lubricants, the mannerisms,
The metaphors, everything! The mission has been aborted.

People, you are no longer a suitable expression
For matter's primordial restlessness. Mom and Pop,
Our glory days are behind us.

Today we uncover the falsehood announced from the
Crow's nest of Noah's ark, or the Pinta, or
Apollo Eleven. Today we uncover the illusion and resign;
Today we burn the tower's last tier.

Novaradock, matter reverting to Eden; who
Else could have been behind the Apple Tree?
Protoplasm retreating from lofty Linnaean orbits . . .
Exalted, unsustainable, hierarchical orbits . . .
Spacious distant and diffused orbits, where
Dizzy astronauts browsed on sunshine,
On power that refused to turn into milk.

Visualize! Tired mouths slur out slogans,
An advantage, obscuring other heights at a time
When beauty is besmirched. Visualize, Novaradock, burnt
Novaradock, her flames could not tip any scales.
Novaradock Capta!
A bronzed plaque nailed down to the pickled ground,
A weightless display flickering on a clear screen.

Today, December fifth, the troops rushed in,
A carbon steel and fury river flowing uphill to drown
The surviving doubts and afterthoughts. And beauty,
Ornamented with play money, stunning, has sailed away
Under a new flag-of-convenience.

Obersturmbannfuhrer Shafer, sturmbannfuhrer Jager,
Sturmbannfuhrer Wiebens: Do we owe you a special
Citation For a job well done in Novaradock?
Einsatzgruppe B (later Changed to C), Einsatzgruppe
C, Einsatzkommando 3 and 8, Special Group citation
For a luminous beacon dedicated, for a milestone
Erected?

A milestone citation for the books, for word-greased
Interim activities, deeds for the ear-littered
Streets, ideals sprung on the unsuspecting;
Nach dem abzug der Rotenarmee(Red Army) hat die
Bevokerung Von Novaradock in einen Spontanen Erhaung
Etwa 2500 Juden(Jews) Erschlage(hit). Eine weitere
Groere anzahl Von Juden is durch den polzeihilfsdienst
(partizanen) erschossen(shot) worden. Jedes(every)
Hause(house) mus(must) vernichted(be destroyed)
Werden, das die besatzungsmachte fremden siedler
(foreign agitators) zuweisen. Zum shlus heist es?
"Es lebe(lives) der Freihitskampf(freedom fight)
Des Novardocker Velkes. Kampf gagen(fight against)
Die Verbrecher(criminals) Mussolini und Hitler!",
From the underground's whispers to reality—Top
Secret, too.

Novaradock, our Novaradock, yesterday and tomorrow
Stood their ground; our idea mongers and yours fuel
Better crematoria fires, waste less motion
In the shooting trenches.

Gimpelovsky, Leibovitch, Ginzburg . . . 6000 today,
The remaining 450 on August, 7th; 100 tunnel
Escapees are unaccounted for.

Aware of other lands that bore our mark, the hidden
Ecosystems we slashed, burned to fatten the land,
Spiked on and on by the common dreams of the herd,
Columbus and Marco Polo wastelands forgot our dreams,
Our prophets have been transcribed without fidelity.

Who can claim the burden of knowledge, who qualifies?

In the competition for substance, Novaradock
Has vanished among the quasars and black holes.
Who will spill blood for Novaradock, when words are
All that is left behind?

Words, a new baseline mark notched on the heart;
A marker to lean into, rotate and push out;
A zero milestone we leave behind; a bloodied
Eden where, this time, our ram failed to arrive.

Be a trust, one more face to trust;
Look under the sandals, darkness and worn leather,
And scared, squeezed space signing off:
"You must kill to eat, burn to eat, rip to eat."

2. My Birthday

On my own since Forty One,
Twelve, five, nineteen forty one,
The fifth anniversary of my Haifa birth,
Free of reason, free to look ahead at last.

I walk along the fence and peek through
At the hard-packed donkey trail, dust to dust.
I marvel at the clarity rushing to my retinas,
Clarity magnified, one thousand to one.

My eyes, high atop a thick-branched mulberry
On the Sharon Plain, swell with color and joy.
I drink and drink my intoxicating presents:
A cool afternoon from the gray mosaic floor tiles,

Scratchy chirps from the squeaky door hinges,
Coos from the pigeons huddled under the eaves,
The sight of the coiled viper cooling
Along the raised pipe in the water meter box,

The painted faces of goldfinch nestlings,
Yellow-smiling blindly at my teasing knuckles.
I've learned to cross the wadi unassisted.
I've learned to stay put, then move on.

Learning is what I do,
And a birthday is an opportunity
To fine-tune the thirsty, sucking horizons,
To set a course and move on, away from set-backs.

Here I enrich my growing collection of thoughts
And began the redistribution of borrowed memories.
My birthday, its edges are rounded by secret
Benefactors; its tears are only for myself.

A fine place to be, two, three child-lengths high,
Atop the heavy middle branch of the mulberry tree.
My eyes color the blue-piped plain
On yellow-clear days and cloud-thick nights.

I look down at the ground
That bears our weight effortlessly,
At the pebbles I dislodge so easily
When my fantasy zig-zags away, touching, skipping . . .

My little steps swell with satisfaction,
And every promise is an accomplishment.
Off the launch pads of Mulberry SpaceCenter,
Zippy party decorations fill the space below

The stars. I trick the slow-dying honey bee
To sting the leaf and pay, and stalk stealthily
The camel caravans carrying inland
The bagged ground seashells dug at the beach.

Here I learned the lessons of exploratory medical
Abrasion taught by eight-year old Lea and her sister,
And the leaps and loops of kitchen dwellers
Catapulted away with mysterious, playful erections.

Here I pitched the tents, drew the battlefields
And dissipated the surges of resolute hormones
Driving my misdeeds. Here I deflated the strength
Of rules, and kept for myself the chosen moments.

Here I first painted distant pictures
In every circle of a turning wheel, and made
Tentative agreements with fear and demons
On long walks along cypress and eucalyptus hedges.

After the rain I dug tunnels and caves
Into the soaked mudwalls of the wadi,
And swam away with the fish that never lived there
And the tall schooners that did.

I tried to ignore the pinch of last year's shoes
And follow the trusty old tracks concealed under
The leafy wild flowers. The arching apple boughs
Dripped annoying rainwater into my collar.

After the rain I waited for the black ants to
Resurface into the bowl of their caldera.
After the rain we bored three dimples in the wet
Sand for the marbles game.

And Saturday was the best day to hear
The slow putputting of a distant water pump.
A fifth birthday in the happy ward of my spaceship.
Curious onlookers press their foreheads against

The window. A gray Spitfire flying by,
Spinning a single red eye; a roofless
Tracked troop carrier, bumping along
In the dust, smelling of petroleum and sausage.

A day of listening to blue-labeled 78's, Chanuka songs,
Oil and miracles in the voice of Bracha Tsfira;
A day when the Past did not intrude and the future
Waited patiently for Mom and Pop to come back from work.

3. Breathing Under Cold Rubble

To scorch the track and advance the desolation,
Regroup and wait for assurances. Rejoin the ranks,
We have done deeds like this before.

The promise is in the deed; a flow of sustenance
To the blind dangling at the end of the diamond-hard
Umbilicus; time has come back again and again, with
Sperm vigor and ovum compassion to compel wisdom
On the believers, who flew into the clouds trusting
A horizon that wasn't there; trusting the seat
Of their pants in the cloud and crashed.

Who will believe the story now, when meaning
Has been laid to rest?

Pricey concessions to timidity, thoughts came forth
Amidst fire. What is Novaradock to you now?
To us, here? A carnival at the season's conclusion?
A minor graveyard slipping under fallen leaves and
Cut flowers?

We can find pearls in oysters miles from the sea
And a hospital with an overworked nurse
At the pulse. Who was in love here before the fire?
Who laid hands on tiny shoulders with passion
And expectations, when the tilted spin and
Imperfections conspired and the core went hot?

The pain has been paid in full, and a new foundation
Sunk into the bulldozed terminal morain.
Novaradock, you separated words from their meaning,
Forever.

Your burnt homes are now burnt homes.
Your shot women are now shot women.
Your body mutilators are now body mutilators.
And your woods are woods with open trenches
Full of people not alive. No. No.

Novaradock, oy, oy, oy, Novaradock has burned,
Oy, oy, oy, what a world? What a world . . .

4. To Open The Book

I began to read among the sounds
Of swollen bodies dragged through brittle snow, and
The tearing-cabbage-leaves sound of an autopsy
In progress. A rhythm came along—losses computed
On knowing peasant fingers and spikes of wheat
and barley nodding in the breeze.

55

Novaradock, collapsing mass has swallowed you,
And shrinking space has closed the hatch on all words
And their embryos. I lift my head up and see
Vistas of smothered grime recede
From the strutting combatants, who spun around
On their heels to face reloaded muzzles.

Tomorrow, December sixth nineteen forty one,
We will recall, with pictures and text, the fifth
Of December—A Day of Summation, the fourth—a Day
Of Despair, the third—a Day of Planning,
The second—a Day of Feeble Arrogance,
The first of December—a Day of Blurred Sweetness.

Tomorrow, while blood hardens in the open, soft
Wintry light will buzz logic and dreams through optic nerves,
and frozen blisters will drip yellow crystals.

Knowledge, who will lay claim to you now? Aleph,
Bet, gimmel, dalet; Abraham cowered,
Bruria bled, Gavriel gave up and David died.

Who will claim sympathy when so much is pending,
When shadows are seen as light by dark-adapted eyes?

Novaradock, economy of deeds and dream;
Lithuanian, Latvian, Belorussian, Russian, Polish,
Karaites, VolgaGerman, Georgian and Estonian deeds
And dreams bled of time to the beat of the Rift
Valley tom-toms throbbing in every cell.

Faith, underwriting every voyage so far, will you
Remain aboard on our way back from Novaradock?
Did you leave behind enough healing
In a mind assembled for high performance? Faith . . .

Devour and shift the costs of runaway desires;
A stone inscribed, a stone unread, formless
In the void, facing the deep dark and the spirit
Moving upon these waters, still untouched.

8/90

II. IF YOU LOVE ME

Choni, The Circle Man

Before Auschwitz and the Great Loss
I went down to the beach
To talk to the fish.

Below the soft brown cliffs,
Choni, the circle man, was drawing
In the sand with his staff.

"One hundred thousand circles from
Haifa to Natanya, and millions* to go;
Shelters for my children," said Choni.

While my eyes, glued to the horizon,
Waited for their arrival, the sand
Under my feet erupted.

Petroleum, cried the fish when
Every circle became a well;
One hundred thousand wells in the sand.

The waves rose high and crashed
Hard against the cliffs
Chasing us from the beach.

"My children . . . they will never come," said
Choni, the circle man,
And drew a circle around us
Atop the soft brown cliffs.

*Millions of Jews were left stranded in Nazi Europe when the British, under Arab pressure, severely restricted the entrance of Jews into Palestine.

10/90

When The Century
Was Three Decades Old

When the century was three decades old
I was ready for the Light
So I went to 15 Meinekestrasse, Berlin,
To hear the news from Zion, the home
Of the Luminous and Merciful.

The dream, I've heard, has come
To a new beginning.

Food—we'll grow;
Roads—we'll build;
Trees—we'll plant;
We will fill in all the squares.

At night Reb Amnon came to me again.
Behold, he said, this is the Day of Judgment;
Every land can eat the people,
And I must die so you can live.

Thankful but confused, I was
At a loss for words when
My feet began to tremble. Oh Love!

I am taking pleasure without going to seed.
Oh, Patria, for your best smile I'll wait.

For your warmth, for your warmth,
Patria, Patria, I'll cash in my time
And stay.

Casablanca, 8/20/89

Within Chronos

We have opened and closed many doors,
But some always stayed shut.
Others, opened so long ago,
Have kept us in, unknowingly.

We can go on and do Better,
But is Worse worth the effort?
Can we pass on, later, that
Which we never put together well?

And why would anybody listen,
If all we did was accept
Reinforcement for our belief
That death is out of the question?

1/2/90

Survival Of The Fittest

When the war broke out, Mrs. Rabbit,
You rushed back from your Baltic-shore,
August vacation to Wilno, and
Into the jaws of the fox and wolf.

When you cut and run to the Russian
Border (to the German border . . . really?)
Did you give thoughts to Darwin and
Process, to races replacing races,
To systems replacing people?

Could you see the adamant ox,
Fighting and losing
At the abattoir's gate?

After two thousand years
In the North,
Could you hear your children,
Walking dazed in the forest, mumbling,
"Life is good here; life is so good."

6/89

Moshe Dayan's Eye

Before the war-to-cleanse-humanity.
Before Birkenau and Bergen-Belsen,
You could watch,
For the price of a beer, a donkey
Mount a woman in Marseille, and
Strangers copulate in Berlin.

Protecting the world's standards,
A French soldier, with his back
To the Rhine, shot out Moshe Dayan's Eye.

1940 was a year to remember.

In New York I hear gypsycab drivers mumble,
Merci beaucoup, merci beaucoup,
Dreaming of gold-leafed caviar canapés
In the back of a limo—*très chic,*
Très chic, but

Looking down into the loaded silos,
I wonder, what will we sacrifice
When the prophets of haut frivolity
Arrange another rendezvous with elegance
For us.

Brooklyn, 1985

Do You See?

Soothsayer, soothsayer,
What do you see now?

Do you see the crowd
Watching the lost hoopoe
Pecking for worms in the grass
Next to the blind man's hut?

Do you see
The baby battalions moving on;
Tiny hearts giving power a chance
To pick a winner?

Do you see
The brightwork fading, the chrome
Removed, and narrow cement-lip overhangs
Rejecting color, closing shut, untouched?

Do you see the wind stop
Shifting moonbeams in the bogs,
Where life's experiments
Fester and ooze?

Yes you, a witness to gray time
East of the Elbe, North of the Source,
Do you see?

Sinking In Haifa Harbor

Boarding measured time, synchronized
Trivia, we hobble aboard. Tired,
Confused, wasted, heavy sledge-
Hammers stamp visas on our backs.

When the orange-laced Gelignite roars
And the vessel sinks, we toss
Our infants overboard, father to
Father, Jew to Jew, before the stern
Jolts the bottom.

Blindfolded, we crawl ashore,
Backbones and wings crushed,
Elbows and knees furrow the sand
Among the dried thistles and stones.

Behind the fences, lottery winners
Dig in; blood monogrammed shovels
Stick to numb and blistered palms.

But the homing comets keep coming in,
Blasting; where are the living waters?

And the rocks, the air, the mist,
The light and thunder respond: stay
Down, at Tranquillity Base,
You have been up long enough.

1985

Adolph & Eva
(and the Mufti of Jerusalem)

This time when the snake spoke
He said, "Light the ovens, Adam,
Eve is naked and freezing.

Trouble? No trouble . . .
Nobody wants the Jews.
The gates to the promised lands
Are closing and the ships are coming back.

You will burn them here,
And we will throw the rest
Into the sea.

11/90

Tamara

When you love me, Tamara,
Whom do you hate?

When you look at his picture,
Lovingly embroidered into your fabric,
One flight above Second Avenue,
Do you see his Cossack shablia
Slash my soft belly?

Can Bogdan Chemielnitcki's ghost,
Fierce, dashing astride his horse,
Ride between your loins and mine
To set our exile ablaze; blood
Splashing in the melee,
Secretions and nostrils frothing,
Limbs thrusting, crumbling aloud?

He will ride again, Tamara;
Trim, arm-banded, exhorting
The yearning of the torch-lit crowd.

He will ride again, Tamara,
For our children's passion;

For their love growing
Along the Unter den Linden,
For their hate crashing
On Friedrichstrasse, spilling away.
He will ride again.

5/87

Herzl's Playmates

We are Herzl's playpen playmates.
Bright-eyed, fresh-smiling Mama's boys,
Waiting for our hot cocoa to cool,
And our creamed banana dessert.

For Mama we went to Yodephet to die,
And returned to Jerusalem Roman scribes.
Angered, we built the Third Wall, then
Sued for peace when the First was breached.

Sweetly we squirm
Under the blank Vespasian gaze,
And delight at the small-screen
Clarity of our toys.

We are Josephus-filtered cafe cruisers
Who never bled for Gush Chalav.

1/2/90

Vienna

I took Vienna with me
To Union Square for
Cupcakes and instant,
And a look at my IOU's.

Tattered negotiables
For millennia of sweet
Church Sundays,
Crumpled and stained bonds
For Karl, Ziggy and Albert,

Convertible pledges for
All the cheeseburgers
I can eat.

To The Drone

To the drone
The spent buzz
Is freedom growing
From the bottom up,
From starvation to plenty
From nothing . . .
To rest outside,
And die on the ground.

Reward! Naked
By the beekeeper's hut,
Tidy storm shelter on the pond,
Adding minutes in the crowd
And riches in the mud.

Reward—to watch
Old acquaintances tinker
With memories of the hive;
To clutch my viscera
And trust the dust.

3/90

Immune Deficiency

Hey, Flying Dutchman!
Your family, yawning in the harbor,
Left you scratched
Where healing is slow,
Where anxious antibodies founder.

How many labyrinths
Did you eagerly hurtle through
Looking for medicine,
To find your blood drying
On the countertop
And the splattered wallpaper
Peeling off? Leaving,

Close your eyes and listen;
Rushing air and water,
Enduring enemies and friends,
Are with you
Forever plummeting into the fog.

Yeshu Over Vitbesk

Pitchforked old-timers stab haystacks,
Earth breasts in chrome yellow,
Earth of darkened clods and winter whites.

Braided, gold-crowned tributes,
A bride and long-baking bread, sigh:
Oh, Mother-in-heaven, open
Your heart to us.

Overhead, the night wings whisper
Thoughts of pure angelic blues,
Chronos touching and teaching,
Yeshu sputtering over Vitbesk.

Butterfly, Butterfly

To you I say: Butterfly, Butterfly, our house,
Kneeling by the heaved and malevolent streets,
Is dividing, almost two.

The angry are out, ready to spoil our fable;
The abandoned, rise from the cracks, yet
The gates are open and innocent.

Jealous eyes, crimson ears, pounce, flatten
The sweet chatter of the parlors,
The love we made in Vienna,
The love we made unloved. Run,

With Moses the Prince, with Ezra the Scribe. Run,
Through forests of raised fists and daggers,
Before our virtues reunite, ablaze,
On the burning altars of the square.

12/89

Visions

The world, crowded into our crania,
Awash with sudden starts and stops,
Is what we have, what will never be.

Truth, vulnerable between dawn and dusk,
Has no past, no future under these lights.

Justice, among us, shamelessly
Victimizes the living
For the sake of the dead,
And soothes the unborn
Very late the morning after.

For this, and other visions,
We'll walk the hot coals again
Ahead of the sweeping mudslide.

1/2/90

Let Us Look

Let us look one more time
Into the mirror
Smoldering in its tracks.

Temptation, a flickering magic lantern,
Squirts promises onto our retinas,
And wisdom, startled,
Leaves our lips flash-distorted
And freeze-fractured.

Can we ask our reluctant coils
To transcribe a cipher
And take matters out of our hands,
To remind us that we
Did not light the Torch,
We only carry it a mile forward;

To warn us that we, beacons
Of weird properties of matter,
Are looking at faces
Lamely sustained by time.

Eyeless

I was stumbling over milestones
When a roadside thistle lashed at me:

"When we remember Zion . . ." you promised,
"If I forget thee Jerusalem . . ." you repeated,
"Let it be written that
They may be destroyed . . ." you ignored.

Before new growth returns to observe,
Before you step between the pillars,

Will you lead the boy to safety;
Will you take him by the hand.

10/23/89

The Promised Land

Promise, you birthed Abraham
Out of his land
To shuttle forever
Between blazing pillars;

The enticing and consuming,
Fore and aft—
A Promise(d) Land,
Can the two be one?

The Land and the Tamarisk,
Can these be one?
Land to walk upon
And shade to rest under
And wait
For the Fire and Ax.

5/89

Deluded

Deluded. I declared myself present,
The hub of the best wires,
Bestowed with a personal destiny,
An independent, vision-gathering singularity.

Thrown together, one of many
Blind combinations of DNA, I kept
Abreast with untried time coming.

Deluded. I looked for solutions and
Ignored the price that tagged along.

I waited for a gleaming likeness
To emerge from the tired, receding swill.

Sheltered. I considered vast plans
To cope with the onslaught, hoping
To barter sleepless nights for
A phantom grip on the tiller and
A resolute forward stare through the haze.

Deluded. I declared a win,
A gain, an end; sanctioned to be
Content among friends while
The wake and the undertow converge.

Home

Away
I learned about home.
The wars
The colorless time
The procrastinating promises
Expelled from
Smoldering landfills.

I came back
To pose
For one more snapshot
Then
I tapped myself shut
In the keg
And let it float
Into the cataract.

David Gimpelovsky,
The Novaradocker Farmer

David Gimpelovsky,
The Novaradocker farmer,
Why are you David
And not Ivan?

    My heart is in the East, but I am
    At the edge of the West, said Halevy.

Release me.
The House of Ishai is burnt,
And too many fine words
Litter the sky.

    How can I taste fine food?
    How can I take pleasure in fields growing?

My sons are strong,
My daughters are beautiful,
And our house
Is waiting to be built.

    I hear a bugle crying and the shuffle
    Of soldiers awakened for the third watch.

Blue-eyed, broad-shouldered,
We can tame
The black spirits
Of the forest.

I dim the light and cover my eyes:
Insanity, stay! Protect me while I am lost.

The stone I swallowed
Never traveled down
To mark days
Of harvest, of departure.

Anger, dubious resident shade,
You have been sold for a pittance.

Naked in the twilight, I draw closer
To the steps I never took; the debt accrued.
You should have died another death, David,
And lived to hear Mickiewitz sing forever,

But you died so young . . .

5/89

In Our Village

In our village
The bulletin board
Does not list
Personal notices anymore.

Newcomers spreading
Familiarity too thin.

Numbers crowding numbers
On the screen,
Styles merge into styles
In the streets, and
Urging cursors cry
Press on, regardless.

Fear

Fear has brought Napoleon
To Vilnius
On his way to Zion.

Fear has kept him
On the road, but
The view was not rewarding.

What is Jerusalem
To Paris eyes?

Fear has brought cold sweat
To Winged Liberty, but
No enduring tyrants to deride.

Fear has kept our dream
Aloft until
We dug our graves in Ponary.

Why is Jerusalem D'Litta
A grave for me?

5/89

When The Vessels Broke

When the vessels broke
I felt the cipher
Pour from the shards—
A sudden change of direction
In the schoolyard.

The code, a personal call to arms,
Instantly grasped by the candidates—
A heart-to-heart infectious sweetener
Arrived to cement our dead ends.

7/89

Huayno

"Hath a nation changed their gods,
    which are yet no gods? But my people have
    changed their glory for that which doth not
    profit."
            Jeremiah 2,11

Walking on marble through the columns,
Robes rustling in the fog, Huascar
Lays a wreath at the foot of the flame.

The Legion honored, the medals tucked
Away among Chanel and Lalique's finest,
Ambassadors ponder the melancholy.

The Sun King, compassionate and graceful
Is reeling-in the cracks. And we, the
Consensus of callous hands and spirits

Crowded shoulder to shoulder, are
Ready to forget the past and
Remember the future. We say,

Inti, speak to us, here and now,
In Quechua. Both banks
Of the river are waiting.

The cannons boom two more salvoes,
And the silver tube swallows
The trunks. He is leaving

For Cuzco, and we, abandoned by
Timelessness and reverie, prepare
To board the Ark again.

Brooklyn, 1985

The Protocols Of
The Congress of Zion

The Covenant, dear brother, is valid,
But it is time to compose a new manifesto;
To paste aristocratic words on parchment
And hoist the banners aloft.

It is time to dig a tunnel
Under the noses of the guards at the gate,
And flow in with the river.

At the bend, the pace will slow down and
The load will settle into a beach.
The ox-bow of tomorrow will be a meadow.

We are cutting from A to B directly.

For four years instead of forty,
The desert will eat the disabled and unfaithful, but
The brave and cunning will take Jericho and spread.

They will rise to the top of the mountain, dear brother,
And come back with the Tablets refurbished,
Pure water, pure water alive for the needy.

Agadir, 8/24/89

Time

What good is the voice
that spoke before
space revealed its
bent secrets
before Big Bang's colors
stopped running
before time said
WHEN I MOVE I'M SPACE
WHEN I REST I'M MATTER

1987

In The Intertidal Zone

In the intertidal zone
The barnacle clings to the rock.

The sun and wind remove the moisture
And the tides bring it back.

Here in the intertidal zone
The future yields no answers

Waiting for the rock
To make its intentions clear.

III. A STORY FOR OUR CHILDREN

Maybe

Maybe it didn't happen.
It couldn't.

Maybe it did not happen
The way it happened.

Maybe it was a European disaster
That spilled into our ghetto.

Maybe we were innocent bystanders
In a clash between giants.

Maybe their giant
Beat our giant.

Maybe it was something
That does happen on the edge.

Maybe it was a mistake;
An inappropriate reaction in a blind turn.

Maybe it was an experiment
That got out of hand.

Maybe time was moving fast
And we tired too soon.

Maybe we became ordinary, commonplace
And useless.

Maybe we are not
What we think we are.

Maybe we are
What they think we are.

Maybe we are both,
And split open too quickly.

Maybe the taxman caught up with us
And we had to pay backtaxes.

Maybe it was a natural phenomenon;
Self-pruning of overgrown, intertwined branches.

Maybe the guidelines lost their urgency
And compliance became too lax.

Maybe we thought too much like one,
After all, and he chose poorly.

Maybe we listened to Moses and Jacob too often
And to Rivka and Rachel not often enough.

Maybe Jonah got out
But the message didn't.

Maybe the message was getting through
But not to us.

Maybe we became genetically vulnerable
Through prolonged inbreeding.

Maybe it was something like Tay-Sachs
But in our perception.

Maybe it was an enlarged spleen,
An enzyme deficiency like Gaucher's disease.

Maybe our immune system faltered
And we developed an inflamed good sense.

Maybe we hoped it will happen to them
Not to us.

Maybe our niche expired, and we
Were too specialized to survive.

Maybe we settled without a fight
Into the comforts of old age.

Maybe we expected perfect vision,
Forever.

Maybe we were too impatient
And tested our creed too soon.

Maybe the fire does consume the bush
In the end.

Maybe we gambled
And lost.

Maybe we had to return home
To revalidate our travel documents.

Maybe the dent we put in the horizon
Weakened the retaining wall.

9/25/89

The Scroll Of Esther

Read the Scroll one more time.
Read the warning
That came without His name,
With the Moses brand scratched out.

There was Mordechai, at the gate,
With his antennae deployed
To listen, to protect, and

Here are we, still clutching
The barren breasts of Liberty,
Of Anarchy, of Movements—
Social and Commune, counting
Six million credits rolling
At the end of our bombed Purim Play.

6/86

100

The Auschwitz Century Games

When we lost our wisdom and faith
We rode with the winners to Olympia.

In Medina, the Magreb and Gaul,
In Spain, Ashkenaz and the North,
We stayed close to the highways
And never raised the flag.

In the Auschwitz Century Games,
When peace and nobility ignited spontaneously
To declare Rome for the Romans,
We could see that stamina and prowess,
Wisdom and faith still counted,
When the winners killed their own
And marched home with gold.

Holocaust

I have been given
An assignment.
Your good
Can be my good.

For that
We have spent
Long and assiduous
Millennia together. Yet,

What has come out
Of that counsel
Behind bars,
Of immovable heads
To immovable heads,
Of unmatched stones
Asunder at the ramparts?

Dreamers, awakened apart,
Prowling around
The discarded wrapper
Of their union,

Flickering remnants
Alone at last,
Sifting through the tailing
Of their vanished
Generosity.

To Run

Sure, the trees will be back
After the ax.
They wait, they stay
Because they must.

To run is our courage,
Why not then?

Shackled to our roots,
We waited;
Caught in the headlights—
Felled and flattened.

Would we try the soil after
Our roots had been exposed;
The air, our grave after the ax?

Would we try the light again
To measure our shadow in the crowd?

La vida es
bastante seria, Moíses

The wolf?
It went that way, Moshe.

The lamb?
The other way.

Mount Sinai?
Burnt down in Auschwitz.

All that is left
Is the Plaza de Toros.

The Plaza de Toros?
This way, Moshe.

Algeciras, 9/4/89

In The Park

In the park I spread
The blanket on the grass
For my children
And our pet fawn to rest.

Thinking of our loved ones' absence,
I could not calm myself.
When the fawn rose to its feet
I cried out:

Look at what had been done to us,
We have been shot, gassed,
Buried bleeding, and
Our remains processed

Into soap and decorations!
They were not moved, except
The boy, who cried because I was upset,
But he soon fell asleep in my arms.

7/89

The Hermit Crab

Magic is sleeping in my classroom.
My words, knots untied from a willing tapestry,
Skim the surface in search of a dry foothold.
Words without a future collapse on the wall
Unstructured, unarrayed, unaccepted.

In a shell laid down to another creature's measurement
A hermit crab is dreaming
Dreams of ill-fitting, irritating contours
Upholstered with borrowed softness.

I do battle with my thoughts
And bring images to the forefront
To let new solutions exhaust their short lives
Before souring into formless curds.

Here, with its umbilical rumble throttled,
Pedagogy is abstaining from deeds.

What else, I wonder, was hiding among the howls and
Lamentations but people down on their luck?
What else was heard when the doors opened
But fugitives rearranging their masters' language?

Growing silver and confused
I watch wavelets erase beached phantoms
From the golden ramp, then
Roll back empty-handed, no wiser than myself,
No wiser than the grown hermit crab
Darting freshly naked from shell to shell
Looking for a suitable home
To rescue from the flooded beach.

Long Ago

On Victory Day '45 memory paused
Under the eucalyptus tree and dropped

A large coin right side up, its brilliance
Laminated under fingerprint fat.

The girl, who pinned a blue and white ribbon
On my shirt, giggled and joined the crowd

At the circle dance, while I
Sought shelter behind the immense,

Whitewashed trunk and waited for
The pitiless procession to get off the road.

10/31/89

A Post Card

With you, the hosts
And us, the guests,
We did all right.

Intimacy would have
Ruined the good times.
We had to refuse.

You became angry,
Violent at your worst—
We could not defend ourselves.

We parted with bad feelings;
Sorry it ended that way.

7/89

Tarifa, Andalucia, 9/5/89

This has been said before,
But since the weight of the Earth
Did not change after millions
Had been gassed in Auschwitz,
It might be worth repeating:
All expressions of self-preservation
Are at the expense of others,
There is no other way.
And while opinions and facts
Are the children
Of sensory input management,
The drive for self-preservation
Would hardly change,
Even if the weight of the Earth did.

Why Can The Engineers

Why can the engineers ride the trains
And come back alive?

Why can the hunters walk
On the electrified ground unhurt?

Border to border, landmark
To landmark, I scrutinize the archives

For clues; I scrutinize my facial tags
For leads; I examine my DNA coils

For reasons, and there, on Adam's
Original manifest, I read the answers:

The engineers can ride the trains
And come back alive; the hunters

Can walk the electrified ground unhurt.

10/4/90

Chasidei Umot HaOlam

A holocaust banished us in,
And a holocaust burnt us out.

In between we lived on the edge,
Always on the edge.

We left behind crumbling synagogues,
Impatient imitators and few
Audacious silhouettes glued
So desperately brittle
To the roaring skyline.

Mostly His Words

In Hiroshima a pope tells the crowd:
We know that in the past
It was possible to destroy a village,
A town, a region, even a country,
But as we can see right here
The whole planet has come under threat.

Now, many years after Auschwitz,
We are ready to face
A basic moral consideration:
From now on
It is only through a conscious choice,
And through our deliberate policy
That humanity can survive
Or perish.

4/89

The Pope And My Mother

The second time the Pope visited my mother
He returned a book borrowed long ago
Before both had left Poland.

Her full breasts renowned in the district,
She read often in the Novaradock woods.
Thirsty, he followed the rumors,
Promising to write children's books
For the many she would have.

He was thirsty now, too,
From the long walk to Segal's orchard.
She was bent over a wild lemon tree stump
Grafting a Shamuti orange to it.

They spoke their own thoughts,
Separated by time, longing to be heard,
Loving the memory of summer smells
Of apples and pears stored in cool cellars.

Growing very old he knew that
He could not write about dying
With wisdom and perspective, so
He promised to write a children's book
Before his powers failed.

Knowing she could not use all the fruit,
Nor keep some children from leaving,
She promised to stay and tend the graves
Of those who died young,
To visit the prisoners and send
Holiday fruit baskets to those who left.

An Evening With Gunter Grass

An evening with Gunter Grass
At the Hebrew Y. May First,
The Eve of Yom HaShoah.

We are given a list of his books:
*Dog Years, Cat and Mouse, The
Flounder, The Rat* . . .

I wonder what is in these books
For the bubbling Germanophiles,
Third-generation Kristallnachters —
These aging orphans.

A German that irritates Germans, he is.
I understand — a good and generous person,
A winner in rumpled clothes,
Speaking a tongue so much like Mother's.

When he reads from *Show Your Tongue*,
He is with the people of Calcutta;
Perceptive of their dignity, assimilating
Their agony into the life of the Grass family —
A hunter's respectful twig-in-the-mouth
Proferred to the fallen Calcuttans.

5/18/89

Wausau

I know our Germans
Beat their Germans,
And our Gypsies, Jews
And deficients live
And theirs burn.

I also know that time
In a deep cave
Flakes away in layers.

So, jogging past Rudi Kron's,
Dieter Stahl's and Fritz Shultz's
Mailboxes,
Lancing watchful gazes
Over the laid out order,
I pick up the pace.

1986, Wisconsin

The Gottleib Daimler Centennial

Inhale the road air
Of Chelmno, Dear Gottleib,
Depravity blended with reason;
Jews auto-da-fe'd on the run.

A German truck, the rolling
Brutality of perfection,
Protecting you, delivering
On time.

$*$ $*$ $*$

And here they come again,
The century models, impeccable,

The fruits of steadfast vision
And uncompromising engineering,
Gottleib Daimler steely babies
For the best among us.

6/86

Teachers, Germans!

Teachers, Germans!
Do you remember
The singed, angry people
Milling about and asking,
"What is wrong with our schools?"
When Sputnik streaked above and America
Toasted eighteen at the Nineteenth?

Nerve gas chemists,
Gas chamber designers,
Crematoria developers,
Death-truck inventors,
Final Solution administrators,
Learned in your classrooms
So what did you ask when . . .

6/86

God Bless You

God bless you, Christians,
You, who consider the skinny,
Nailed down Jew, your Lord.

Oy, such admiration!

You blew it
For a while
With those gas chambers.
Can't be forgiven. But

Babies are born every second
Into the shrinking wards,
Ready to make new mistakes. So

If you must franchise
The Promised Land
To the lambs, we
At the Museum say, again,
God bless you.

The Auschwitz Convent

Gild the domes in the sky.
Stack up the skulls in the cellar.
Fill the gift shop shelves
With bottled ashes and tattooed lampshades.

We have seen it all before:
Muhammad's horse ascends to heaven
From the ruins of our temple,

Monks peddle toy tablets
And fireproof bushes
On the slopes of Mount Sinai.

Muted doggedness moves in
To places vacated by God and evil;
Persistence replaces inspiration.

9/20/89

Hirshl The Plowman

Long before mortgage payments
To the Brooklyn Savings Bank;
Long before the Buick with power steering
And Lou Gehrig's disease,
Hirshl the plowman lost his beasts and land.

What do you do with two strong hands?
What do you do with an iron jail key
As long as an arm, as thick as a thumb?

You sink it into the Polack's skull,
That's what you do; the scum
Who ate at your table at harvest,
The drunk who pissed a full bladder
On your sister's body rotting

In the street. You bury it deep
Into his skull, where it belongs.

12/5/89

My Last German Grand Prix

For Herschel Grynzspan

The eyes, the eyes, white-heat tattoos
Searing recalcitrant tracks through
The Black Forest's forbidding dioramas.

I drive with my eyes nailed to their sockets
Aware of the Big Prize,
A total-rot metastasis
Fouling the water supply.

Onward, rushing at the limit,
I clip perfect-arc inscriptions
On the blind, slippery curves.

Deep inside my occipital screening center,
A cleaner-burning fire
Crackles benedictions when I down-
Shift gears for the final rise . . .

Out of gas, Christ! I thumb
A midnight ride to the filling station
With the headmaster and his bride.

Walking back, can in hand,
I abandon the road when I hear
The ticking jeers of silenced machinery
Laughing at the beaten beggar
And his long-imprisoned specter—
Funerary flames coming home
To the fenced-in dormitory
With the open gate.

1986

Katzetnicks

Hey nurse!
I am here
Many years later,
To be in their company,
To see.

Visions stretched
Thin and brittle;
Pain dragging through chaos
Becoming an affliction;
Desire slowly slipping away
From overheated minds . . .

And nurse, take this cordless
Telephone to them,
My number already dialed in.

I want to be in touch
When clarity,
A fleeting neural reprieve,
Arrives.

1985

By Accident

In the library
By accident
I sat next to
A black woman reading
A book about A. Hitler
And writing a paper
For a teacher who
By accident, is alive.

Silence

Seven survivors play cards
Around the table
Hoping to be dealt a better hand.

All around, mirrors,
Silvered from the outside,
Glitter and shine
Reflecting unabsorbed pain.

Wilted gazes
Shuffle a new deck
For impatient young jacks,
But under the silent slogans
The frost of '44 crackles.

How long into the night
Will the stowaway loiter
Before the last hand is dealt?

1985

Displaced Person

I wait for the sadness
To become a blur. I wait
For the future to settle in
And run the next rerun on fast forward.

The days are without pay
And the nights, a dry-lung scream
Of striped skeletons marching
To the next bite
Left uneaten by the herdsman's dogs.

Move on! Move away!
Do not scare our children in the woods.
Here, we are the victims, the survivors . . .

Take with you the scrolls and icons,
Take away the soap, the lampshades,
The silvery amalgams, the eyeglasses frames . . .

I break the surface in the midst
Of event-infested prosaic time,
Panicked time that isn't mine.

I join the winners in the sidewalk cafe
To watch the popping white light frenzy
Freeze the swollen neurons of the passing crowd
And wait for uncertainty with relief.

5/89

Ten Years Flashed

Ten years flashed
From Munich to Birkenau,
Four years
From crystals to ashes.

Regulars from the newest
Yeshiva on Ocean Parkway
And indoor mall in Ramat Gan
Are squaring off again
Farther from the ground
Within the picker's reach.

12/88

Natanya, Hometown

When Herbert Samuel become High Commissioner
Main Street, Natanya was renamed in his
Honor, and an obelisk was erected
To commemorate the change.

When the gates to the land closed
For the dispossessed and doomed, we
Extended Main Street into the sea
And stenciled Aliya Street on the walls
To welcome the Illegals.

When Herzl's bones flew overhead
On the way to interment in Judea,
Main Street became Herzl Street and
We moved on to new places, relieved.

Between Christmas and New Year's, after
Bavaria and Saltzburgh receded with the contrail
The air approaching the Airbus is restless
And the seatbelt sign chimes on.

Thessaloniki below broods vacant ambivalence,
And I, anticipating an anxious arrival
At the wheel of a rented car, weigh the odds of
A renamed Main Street on the road ahead.

2/89

Behind Shlesinger
In A Yellow Harvard

I am in a yellow Harvard
Behind Shlesinger, the child
Himmler did not gas,

The flier, who died
In the sand when
The Sinai reinstated the pledge.

We are Barak
Releasing light above Jezreel;
We are Elijah

Kindling sonic anger
In the Carmel; we are Samson
Repudiating Satan in Ekron.

We move our time.

To erase the memory of the Big Blunder
Shlesinger spreads ashes
Along our low, thunderous trail,

And I, remembering my father's afternoons
On Olives Mountain, apply black ink
To the letters of our faded deed.

2/89

The Title Search

But the Jewish nation has already
done this kind of one-man show.
Amos Oz

Overheard outside Crematorium # 2, Himmler to Höss:
Who is not a winner here?
Who is a relative and who is a guest?
Who is not a visitor to Plymouth Rock, to Ayers Rock?
Who is not a petitioner at Tenochtitlán? Agreed . . . ?
Then let power stand on its own,
Let silence blow clear through the flue,
And let a mind be a mind and weigh.

Here we are, the impoverished of deeds,
Trembling and frightened, tugging at plans
Tucked away in our traveler's sash.

With pride we wave the colonial extension of our lease
And watch our own musky squirt arch thinly
In the sun toward a higher mark on the fence.

On piles of prefabricated house sections we squat
And admire subterranean opportunities lying fallow.
Opportunities to reroute our facial etchings
For a clearer definition from the second strike
Of the die—words before a roof—

130

Words for renewed feelings; for higher combinations
Of places and spirit to take on time, change arrival
Into a celebration and then, wait for the inevitable
drift closer at the land office files.

Think of this, in the absence of will
An enclosed space full of nitrogen atoms
Will not take in more nitrogen,
But oxygen atoms and others will be welcome.
Cross-bred or isolated,
Relatives or guests, to stay on or leave,
When is the decision made? Still,

In the midst of the relentless sweep of the gradient,
Pulling down, pulling in, stinging,
Dissipating the power of choice, the desire
To light a new light in the sky is undiminished.

When compelling gazes explode off the blocks,
We pierce the starting line painted on our toes
To set off new working definitions
For the scars and imperfections we carry,
For the commandments we struggle with.

But when differences all around us muddle and decay
Whose anxiety will soar higher?

Before words, before rationality,
Similarities walked free among us;
Burnt-in similarities of our helical heritage
Helped our forefathers to communicate,
To attain a simultaneous grasp of the moment—
An understanding—but lost in our vast cocoon of words, with
Cause-and-effect irrigating our gray cells intermittently,
We looked for little things to give us big answers,
Allowing our wisdom and vision to uncouple.

When others imposed restrictions to widen the breach,
We, too, added restrictions to keep ourselves different.

When some felt they must kill to restore their purity,
We felt we must die to restore our purity in His eyes.

When we exposed our jugulars to Him with humility,
Provoking rumors of a deathwish, of an invitation to slaughter,
It became clear that under the baited illumination
Of our fissured lobes,
Even large creatures can disappear behind small neurons.

So when the names on the parchment failed,
And the process failed,
And failure itself lost its fair standing with the living,
We returned to the valley,
Where the hot wind blows fifty days and fifty nights.

We returned to sprinkle fresh spices and pure frankincense
On the patient bones.
We returned with the magic still buzzing inside.

We returned to stand on the promontory and declare: Here I am

9/88

At Rachel's Garden

I am at Rachel's Garden
Below the level of the sea
To hear the palms sing the maker's song
And taste the sweetness of dreams that took root.

I am here to remember the foul vapors of the North
That brought seeds to this valley
And to thank my forefathers
Who died young nursing the psalms of utopia
Into my agenda of renewal.

With my ear to the grass I listen
To the clamor of climbers ascending
The rainless hills. Gordon's foundlings,
Tablets strapped to their foreheads,
Securing a foothold among boulders and thistles
For the topsoil and seedlings they carry.

Your garden is growing, Rachel. Your song,
Fertilizer spread over yesterday's battlefields,
Is yielding to the crash of combatants advancing
With the pin pulled out
For the taste, for the sugar,
For first-fruit tremors throbbing once again.

Marching On

She was cut loose. Young,
With us inside her,
A Polish peasant alone in the desert
Two thousand miles from home.

I came before the fire and confusion.
Her first,
The last one to be awarded
A reprieve.

Out of place in the wilderness,
Her solutions failed;
Out of date,
When her source was silenced.

Lost. Her solutions
Became my solutions; second hand,
Marching on to third.

7/89

Vu Zinen Mine Kinder?

Did she think about the old country today?
Where printers and pharmacists were uncles,
And Grandfather, the peasant of the family,
Grew strong cutting wood and plowing fields,
His yellow cheese wheels, *un calandario Polonés*,
Keeping time in the cellar, aromatically.

Did her heart leap out of her chest
At the end of the long spiral climb
To the peek of Adam Mickiewitz's Hill.
(Yes, Adam is a Russian poet now.)

Does she imagine deep snow on the ground
And winter wheat safely covered, dreaming?

Does she imagine fragrant summer fields,
Where life became a contest,
Big guns flashing, illuminating empty stork nests
Of a distant, flightless autumn.

This time kings and mystics couldn't stop
The rolling, shadowless intruders; perfect
Black bodies and carbon steel delivering . . .

Steady through the chant: Shema . . .

Older sister decomposes on the road. Think
Of possibilities for her body, as the third
Day peers through the shutters, and
Two drunks empty their bladders to douse the stench.

A late, wistful gaze of bright eyes growing dim.
Time for tears for people and places; elocution
From a creaking seamstress trickle in a broken cadence.

Relieved, she mends.

Over borders dripping with pus and melancholy
A hero stallion gallops. Up, up her eyes
Shift to catch darting hoof glints,
Starry remnants of a time compound
From the pharmacist's niece, for our ills.

A Story
For Our Children

To lessen the
Confusion

Should we
Erect

A tower
Of simple
Strengths

Reaching
The sky

For
Young eyes
To look
Down
Safely

And see
Our
flaccid
Weaknesses
Litter
The ramparts?

Babi Yar

Next year
We could have goose liver
In the park,
And maybe *futbol* and parades
If they cut down
Some of the trees.
But today, Yurinka,
We stay with the fog,
Indoors,
Away from October leaves
Sailing down
To the ground,
Matting down
On the ground,
So far from
The memories below.

Keena

And my heart,
Does it not vibrate?
Does it not send out quanta
To battle the chilling aliens
From Broca's world?

Confidently marching paradoxes,
Dichotomies in progress,
Accusing, usurping, defeating.

The flames are here!
Shaking and releasing,
Homim u'vochim,
Unnamed, unclassified, wordless—
The forgotten begetters.

Ashkava

A soldier died yesterday and is buried today.
The skinny girl, who will graduate high school
With cold tears, is crying.

Here we are Sara, the survivors,
Singing songs of hope for your children.
We tear our uniforms midway through the chant
And shoot the blanks into the ground,
A soldier's dowry.

Time, at times like this, needs a rest.

Ancient words stir our emotions;
He is dead and we must live
And follow the tracks — our tracks.

Questions. Answers.
Yesterday's flowers wilting seedlessly
And the night sperm, again, penetrates nothing.

So pick up a stone, a traveler's mat,
And cover the flag,
Dead soldiers make their own arrangements,
And for us a bus and a hot meal are waiting.

If You See Moshe

If you see Moshe tell him
I am stuck in the sand.
The wheels are spinning,
The tires are smoking
And the jack is bent.
Tell him
I don't have any new ideas,
And I must shut off the engine
To give us a rest. I will
Restart in the morning, God willing.

Turning

Stones chip the staff I carry,
A dizzy, spinning propeller
Turning time into distance,

Turning over mildew-prone Spanish
Chestnuts on a steamer journey
From Tetuan to Manaus,

Turning clanging semaphore arms
For a Lithuanian train coming to
Poised Dynamite under the rails' joint.

A practiced Cessna nudges the Hudson River,
Western border of the patched greeting card below;
From Brookhaven to Poughkeepsie, emeralds and opals
Swaddled by the passing cloud slivers.

Under the roofs, stuffed turkeys
Are carved by second wives and new children.

Families recline on pillows that wore out
Sooner than the sandals; families mourning
The hay left to rot in the fields
And the fading tans of summer.

Thanksgiving is spreading under the wing.
Empty seatbelts rest at my elbow;
Guidance taken away from eyes
Looking for the shy road incognita.

On another journey, oceans away,
Breath, anticipating new ripples
On the plate below, flutters in midair.

Another trip from Jerusalem to Granada arising,
Another chance for memory and mercy to embrace.

8/87

The Blade

There, after the rains,
A sharp blade carved
When our river ran dry.

The blade carved and
Did not rust
With moisture and time.

There, after the rains,
The trees grew taller
With moisture and time.

A Family Lost

I count the heads everyday,
Contemplating the replacements
That emerged from the furnace of the past.

Crowded into my commemorative space,
Into Friday night's candle lit wedding,
They came. Kinsfolk, playmates and teachers—
Are they my family?

Yes. Possibilities lost are bartered
For sights to see and time to heal;
Resurrected vistas set to paper,
Gray, to black, to white, to gray.

6/30/89

Sheep

A long time ago it was decided
That sheep would turn into
Army ants and lemmings
And meet at the door
Of the gas chamber.

Good Germans, good Jews,
Splinters of God's only flame,
Pondered the scales, weighed
Their fortunes, their dreams
Of steel and stone, and
Came to the door, the
Crossing of the righteous paths.

And the door, which did not
Fail to open and close, to
Seal in the gas, the panic,
The cries, the terror, is waiting

For trial and error to resume,
For delusion of ingenuity to rise,

And ashes, all ashes,
To make God whole again.

At Xel-Ha

After her husband and son
Snorkeled away,
The woman visitor to my rock
Said, "Rilke? He is good,
But Goethe is our best,
We had to memorize
Him in school."

The book,
Now just paper
Between my fingers.

"Your breasts are beautiful,"
I said.
"Sank you, but I sink
Zey are all ze same."

Notes

"Behind The Door": A "Gauleiter" was a top political leader in the occupied German territories.

"Cloudseeding": "chuppa", a canopy held above the bride and groom in a Jewish wedding; "spermatids" are immature, non-motile sperm cells.

"Sonderkommando": inmate orderlies who did all the physical work, e.g. carrying bodies from the gas chamber to the crematorium, in the German killing camps.

"Thessaloniki Kaput": Thessaloniki, a Greek seaport, whose very large Jewish population was shipped to Auschwitz and killed.

"El Tango Fabuloso": about 90,000 Jews were shot in "Ponary", a wooded recreational area south of Vilnius.

"Judenrat": Jewish civic councils set up by the Germans to facilitate the killing process; the Soviets exterminated large numbers of "kulaks", Ukranian peasants, before the war; "Birkenau", the killing center of Auschwitz.

"Judenrat(2)": some human fat was used by the Germans to "saponify", make soap.

"Seven Portholes In Hell": "psia krew" and "chulera" are Polish profanities.

"Leibel Gimpelovsky": He and three other partisans were shot by the Germans while collecting food from Polish villagers.

"Reb Nachman's Chair": Rabbi Nachman of Breslov, an early Hassidic leader who wrote the song "A Narrow Bridge". During the war his chair was smuggled to Palestine.

"An Astronomer's Lament": The "red shift" of the expanding universe was discovered by the American astronomer Hubble.

"Jack-In-The-Box": "come shot", a filmmaking term for ejaculation.

"Orphans": "Jucha" and "Baba Yaga" are figures from Arab and Polish folklore; "Ashkenaz", Hebrew for Central Europe and Germany.

"A Scroll Concealed": "Ravensbruck", a German concentration camp for women, where inmates were subjected to brutal medical experiments; the "Killing City", a poem by H. N. Bialik, about the pogrom in Kishinev, Moldavia; "Musa Daag", a mountain in Turkey where the Turks massacred thousands of Armenians; "Yosarian", the flier from Joseph Heller's *Catch 22*; "hippocampus" is the site of emotional activities in the brain; "Monte Casino", Italy, where the Germans halted the Allied advance in 1943; "theta wave", the main electrical brain wave; In order to reclaim his inheritance, Jacob had to cross the "Yabok" River and face his brother Esau.

"Relay": Judean captives were brought to Rome through the "Via Appia", the Appian Way; "desert varnish" covers desert stones after long exposure to the sun; "Sellah", a Psalmic punctuation word.

"Polish Transit": In his "Guide for the Perplexed" Maimonides established guidelines for Jewish daily life.

"Look, Look, Look": Our world, the physicists say, may have as many as ten dimension, six more than the traditional four.

"On Kiddush HaShem": Hebrew for God's martyrdom.

"Two Days Before Pearl Harbor": "Entropy", the natural quality of disorder; "Linnaeus", the Swedish botanist who developed the system of biological classification; "Obersturmbannfuhrer" and "Sturmbannfuhrer", German SS ranks for Colonel and Major; "Einsatzgruppe" and "Einsatzkommando" German military killing units established to carry out the activities of the Final Solution; The German Interim Reports cited here are from Y. Arad, S. Krakowski and S. Spector, *The Einsatzgruppen Reports*; "aleph, bet, gimmel, dalet," are the first four letters of the Hebrew alphabet; "Bracha Tsfira", an Israeli singer of children's songs; "formless in the void . . .", Genesis 1,1.

"Choni, The Circle Man": An early Jewish mystic, who advocated improving the world for the coming generations.

"Moshe Dayan's Eye": "Bergen-Belsen", a large German killing center.

"Sinking In Haifa Harbor": Born aboard the S.S. Pacific, Miriam Torren was tossed overboard from the ship which was scuttled in order to avoid deportation from Palestine; "Gelignite" is a plastic explosive.

"Adolph & Eva(and the Mufti of Jerusalem)": The "Mufti of Jerusalem", a prominent Moslem clergyman who supported Adolph Hitler and spent the war years in Berlin.

"Tamara": "Bogdan Chemielnitcki", a Ukranian General and national hero, who perpetrated many pogroms; "shablia" is a Cossack sword; "Unter den Linden" and "Friedrichstrasse" are streets in Berlin.

"Herzl's Playmates": "Yodephet", a Jewish fortress under the command of Josephus, that surrendered to the Romans; "Gush Chalav", a Jewish fortress that did not surrender to the Romans.

"Yeshu Over Vitbesk": "Yeshu", Hebrew for Jesus: "Over Vitbesk", a painting by Marc Chagall.

"Fear": "Jerusalem D'Litta", a name, coined by Napoleon, for Vilnius.

"When The Vessels Broke": A Kabbalistic name for the momentous event that resulted in the beginning of the world as we know it now.

"Huayno": An Andean song form known for its melancholy and purity; "Huascar", the last Inca; "Inti", the Sun God.

"Maybe": "Tay-Sachs" and "Gaucher's" became "Jewish" genetic diseases through centuries of inbreeding among Eastern European Jews.

"La vida es bastante seria, Moíses": Spanish, life is very serious, Moses.

"Chasidei Umot HaOlam": Hebrew, the Righteous Gentiles who risked their lives to help the Jews during the war.

"An Evening With Gunther Grass": "twig-in-the-mouth", is a German hunting custom.

"The Gottleib Daimler Centenial": In the killing center of "Chelmno" sealed trucks were used to deliver Jews, killed with the truck's own exhaust gas, to the mass burial fields.

"Teachers, Germans!": "The Nineteenth Hole" is a bar next to a golf course in Brooklyn.

"Hirshl, The Plowman": Hirshl Gimpelovsky, farmer and partisan, was fired from his guard position in a Soviet jail after he killed a former neighbor for abusing his sister Dinnah's corpse lying in the street in Novaradock.

"My Last German Grand Prix": When "Herschel Grynzspan" shot a German official before the war the Germans retaliated with the Kristallnacht pogrom.

"Katzetnicks": Concentration camp inmates.

"The Title Search": "The impoverished of deeds . . ." from Hineni, the prayer of the Chazzan before Mussaf on Yom Kippur.

"At Rachel's Garden": "Rachel", an Israeli poet; "Gordon" A.D., an early Zionist philosopher who advocated the fusion of Socialist Zionism with Jewish traditions.

"Vu Zinen Mine Kinder?": Yiddish for "Where are my children?";

"Shema", Hebrew for "Listen", the seminal Jewish appeal to the Creator.

"Babi Yar": A ravine where the Jews of Kiev were shot and buried.

"Keena": Hebrew, lament; the speech center in the left hemisphere of the brain has been named "Broca's" area after its discoverer; "nomim u'vochim", Hebrew for moan and cry.

"At Xel Ha": A beautiful salt water cove in Yucatan, Mexico.